Usain Bolt

The Biography of the Fastest Man that Runs Faster than Lightning

By United Library

https://campsite.bio/unitedlibrary

Introduction

Do you want to know who the fastest man in the world is?

Usain Bolt has been breaking records for years and is known as the fastest man that has ever lived. He is a Jamaican runner who holds world records in both the 100 meter and 200 meter dash.

Usain Bolt is a Jamaican sprinter and considered to be the fastest person in the world. He clocked in at 9.58 seconds in the 100-meter race, making him the first man to run the distance in under 10 seconds. In addition, he also holds the world record for the 200-meter race with a time of 19.19 seconds. But Bolt is more than just a fast runner; he's also an Olympic champion.

Bolt has won eight gold medals in total, six of which are Olympic golds. In addition to being an incredible athlete, Bolt is also known for his fun-loving personality and his love of dancing. He often celebrates his wins with his signature "Lightning Bolt" pose, and he loves to show off his moves on the dance floor. Whether he's setting records or entertaining crowds, Usain Bolt is truly a one-of-a-kind athlete.

In this biography, you will learn everything there is to know about this incredible athlete. You will find out what makes him so fast, how he became one of the best runners in history, and what his plans are for the future. If you are a fan of running or just want to learn more about one of the greatest athletes in history, then this book is perfect for you.

Table of Contents

Usain Bolt

Usain Bolt (Sherwood Content, parish of Trelawny, Jamaica, August 21, 1986) is a Jamaican former professional athlete. He holds eleven world and eight Olympic titles as a sprinter, and also holds the world records in the 100 and 200 m sprint, and the 4×100 relay race with the Jamaican team. He is one of only seven athletes in history to have won titles in the youth, junior and senior categories. He is known as "Lightning Bolt".

At the 2002 World Junior Championships, he won a gold medal in the 200 m sprint, making him the youngest winner in the history of the event for that time. In 2004, at the Carifta Games, he became the first junior sprinter to run under 20 seconds in the 200 m, clocking 19.93 seconds, which surpassed the previous record held by Roy Martin by two tenths of a second. His professional career began in 2004, and although he competed in the Olympic Games that year, he would miss the following two seasons due to injuries. In 2007 he broke Don Quarrie's Jamaican 200 m record with a time of 19.75 seconds.

In 2008 he achieved his first world record in the 100 m sprint with 9.72 s, and culminated the year with other absolute records in the same event in the 200 m and in the 4×100 relay race with the Jamaican team, with records of 9.69 s; 19.30 s; and 37.10 s respectively, during the Beijing Olympic Games. Such feats consecrated him as the first athlete to win three Olympic events since Carl Lewis in 1984. In 2009 he broke his own 100 and 200 m sprint records with times of 9.58 and 19.19, respectively, during the Berlin World Championships, making him the first athlete to hold the 100 and 200 m sprint world titles at both the World Championships and the Olympic Games. The time with which he lowered the world record in the 100 m in 2009 is the largest margin since digital measurement was implemented.

At the London 2012 Olympic Games, on August 11, he set a new world record in the 4×100 meter relay with a time of 36.84 seconds. He also broke the Olympic record in the 100m sprint after winning the final with a time of 9.63, setting the best mark in history, and his triumph in the 100m made him the first athlete to win the Olympic gold medal in two consecutive games in both events.

In the 2013 and 2015 world championships, he won three gold medals in each one, which, added to the five won in 2009 and 2011, made him the biggest winner in the history of the event with eleven gold medals. Another milestone in his career was set at the Rio de Janeiro 2016 Olympic Games when he won three gold medals for the third time, but this achievement was marred by the withdrawal of the gold medal in the 4 × 100 m relay in 2008 when it was found that one of the team members had failed a doping test.

After his retirement as an athlete he tried to forge a career in soccer. In August 2018 he was on trial with the Central Coast Mariners reserve team in the Australian league, but failed to reach an agreement on a contract and six months later announced his retirement.1His prowess in sprint events has earned him the nickname *Lightning Bolt*, and the accolades of "Athlete of the Year" from the IAAF, and *Track and Field* magazine, as well as the Laureus award.

First years

Usain Bolt was born in Sherwood Content, a small town in the parish of Trelawny, Jamaica, where he grew up with his parents, Wellesley and Jennifer Bolt, and his siblings Sadeeki and Sherine. His parents ran a store in the rural area where Bolt spent his time playing cricket and soccer with his brother. In fact, he would recall those years with these words:

As a child he attended Waldensia School, and it was there that he began to showcase his sprinting skills, as he ran in the annual school event at primary level in the parish of Trelawny. In fact, at the age of twelve he became the fastest runner in his school in the 100 m sprint.

When he entered William Knibb High School, he continued to concentrate on sports. His speed on the field was already noticed by his cricket coach, who recommended that he take up athletics. It was former Olympic sprinter Pablo McNeil, - with the help of Dwayne Barrett - who began training him to develop his athletic skills. That educational institution had had success in athletics with previous students, including sprinter Michael Green. In 2001, Bolt won his first medal in the high school collegiate event with a silver medal in the 200 m with a time of 22.04 seconds. Following this achievement McNeil became his head coach and would sustain a good friendly relationship with the boy, although he was occasionally frustrated by his lack of dedication and penchant for practical jokes.

First competitions

In the same year, the promising young athlete began to participate in international events. At the Carifta Games she was part of the Jamaican team and achieved a personal best of 48.28 s in the 400 m dash, winning a silver medal. In the 200 m he also won another silver medal with a time of 21.81 seconds. In addition, he had his first experience in a world event during the World Youth Championships in Debrecen (Hungary) and although in the 200 m sprint he could not qualify for the final, he set a new personal best of 21.73 sec.

However, despite the international exposure, the young man still did not take athletics seriously. Proof of this was his childish behavior when he once hid in the back of a van, precisely on the day he was to take part in the 200 m final of the qualifying trials for the Carifta Games. The prank cost him dearly, as he was apprehended by the police while his coach was reproached by the public. However, the incident did not go any further, and they both traveled to the Carifta Games where he set championship records in the 200 m and 400 m with records of 21.12 s and 47.33 s, respectively. Subsequently, he set other records of 20.61 s and 47.12 s in both events in the Central American and Caribbean finals in the junior category.

Already at that time, Prime Minister Percival James Patterson recognized the young man's talent and arranged for him to settle in Kingston with Jermaine Gonzales to train with the Jamaica Amateur Athletic Association (JAAA) at the University of Technology.

Leap to fame

The 2002 World Junior Championships, which took place in Kingston, Jamaica, gave Usain Bolt the opportunity to show his attributes before the international gaze. He was 15 years old and approximately 1.94 m tall, which made him stand out among his teammates. In that event he won the 200 m with a time of 20.61 s; 3 hundredths slower than his personal best of 20.58 s that he had set in the first round; but the victory consecrated him as the youngest to win a gold medal in the junior category in history up to that moment.

Although the experience made him nervous (to the point of putting his shoes on the wrong feet), it paid off in the end, as he determined that he would never again be affected by pre-race anxiety. In addition, as a member of the Jamaican relay team, he won two silver medals and set two junior records in the 4 × 100 m and 4 × 400 m events with times of 39.15 s and 3:04.06, respectively.

The medals continued to pile up, as he would go on to win four gold medals at the 2003 Carifta Games, and claim the "Austin Sealy" trophy for the most outstanding athlete of the games. He also won another gold medal at the 2003 World Youth Championships in Athletics, and set a new tournament record in the 200 m with a time of 20.40 s, despite a 1.1 m/s headwind. Michael Johnson, world record holder in the 200 m sprint, realized his potential, but believed the young man could be under pressure, although he said it would all depend on what he did over the next five years. These achievements had impressed the highest authorities in athletics, for which he received the award for the best young athlete of the year 2002.

Later, Bolt put all his interest in the 200m. In this event he equaled Roy Martin's junior mark with a time of 20.13 s at the Junior Pan American Championships. That result attracted the attention of the sports press, and due to his performance in the 200 and 400 m, he was nominated as the possible successor of Michael Johnson. In fact, at the age of sixteen he had achieved marks that Johnson had not registered until he was twenty years old, and his mark in the 200 m was superior to that of Maurice Greene in the same season.

In his last Jamaican high school championship in 2003, he broke personal records in the 200m and 400m with times of 20.25sec and 45.30sec, respectively. In those races he had set better marks than the previous ones, which exceeded the 200 m by half a second and the 400 m by almost a second.

Meanwhile, the young man was growing in popularity in his country, and Howard Hamilton himself, Jamaica's attorney general, asked the JAAA to strengthen his health and avoid fatiguing him. He also called him "the best sprinter the island has ever produced". However, the fame and attractions of the capital city Kingston began to become a setback for the young athlete. Bolt became careless about his career, preferring to eat fast food, play basketball, and party in the city's nightclubs; and in the absence of an orderly routine, he began to rely on his natural talent to beat his competitors.

As the 200 m champion in both the world youth and junior championships, he was confident of winning the event at the 2003 world championships in Paris. In fact, he had beaten all his competitors in the qualifying events, but he was realistic in his odds and reasoned that, even if he did not make the final, he would consider a personal best as good. However, he suffered a setback when he became ill with conjunctivitis before the event, so his training schedule was completely disrupted. Realizing that he would not arrive in peak physical condition, the JAAA barred him from the championships on the grounds that he was too young and inexperienced. Bolt was demoralized at missing out on the opportunity to participate in the event, but worked hard to improve his fitness to earn a spot on the Olympic team. Nevertheless, he was again recognized as the best junior athlete of 2003.

Professional Career

Beginnings (2004 - 2007)

Under the guidance of his new coach Fitz Coleman, Bolt began his professional career in 2004, and his first competition was at the Carfta Games in Bermuda. There he became the first junior sprinter to run the 200 m under 20 seconds, setting a new record with a time of 19.93 seconds. In addition, he was again awarded the "Austen Sealy" trophy as the best athlete of the event. A hamstring injury almost prevented him from attending the World Junior Championships that year, but he was selected for the Jamaican Olympic team. He went to the Athens Olympics full of confidence and with a new record to his credit. However, a leg injury prevented him from running to his full potential and he was eliminated in the first round of the 200 m with an opaque time of 21.05 seconds. The hard training of those years seemed to affect him, which added to his scoliosis and a shorter right leg.

Still, collegiate institutions in the United States offered him athletic scholarships based on his remarkable performance, but the young man from Trelawny Parish turned them all down, claiming he was content to remain in Jamaica. Instead, he chose the environs of the University of Technology as his training ground, despite the antiquated gymnasium and worn-out athletics track he had used since his amateur years.

In 2005, Bolt began working with his new coach Glen Mills, which would be followed by a change in his attitude towards athletics. Mills knew of the athlete's potential and was determined to change any type of behavior away from his profession; also took him to consult with the German doctor Muller-Wolhlfahrt for treatment of scoliosis, and since then he began to overcome the disorder. The preparation began for the following season, in which he would have as teammates experienced sprinters such as Kim Collins and Dwain Chambers, and by the month of July he would beat the 200 m mark by a third of a second at the Central American and Caribbean Championships with a time of 20.03 seconds, and later established his personal best of the year in the same event in the city of London (England) at Crystal Palace, stopping the clock in 19.99 seconds.

However, misfortune struck once again at the 2005 World Championships in Athletics. Prior to the event, Bolt knew that his personal and sporting work had improved since the 2004 Olympic Games, and he considered that he would meet the public's expectations at the world championships; he himself stated that he wanted to surpass what happened in Athens. In fact, he qualified for the final of the 200 m with a time of less than 21 seconds, but suffered an injury during the race and finished in last place with a time of 26.27 seconds.

In short, injuries prevented him from completing the season, so the young man did not have the opportunity to show his talent in professional events. To make matters worse, he was involved in a traffic accident in November, and although he suffered only scratches to his face, his training schedule had to be modified.

His manager Norman Peart changed the young athlete's regular training to a less intense one. Bolt gradually recovered his level and became one of the top five athletes in the world in 2005 and 2006. In addition, Peart and Mills considered training him over longer distances, so they planned to make the 400 m his primary event between 2007 and 2008. Bolt, on the other hand, was not entirely enthusiastic, and made it clear that he felt more comfortable at shorter distances.

In March 2006, another hamstring injury prevented him from competing in the Melbourne Commonwealth Games, and he was unable to run until May. Once recovered, he underwent further training exercises to improve his flexibility, and plans for the 400 m were put on hold.

When he returned, the 200 m remained his primary event; and to prove it he beat Justin Gatlin in Ostrava (Czech Republic) with a new course record. Bolt was aiming to run under twenty seconds and set a new personal best, but was satisfied with the victory considering that the weather had prevented him from performing well. Nevertheless, he recorded a sub-twenty-second time at the Grand Prix in Lausanne (Switzerland) with a time of 19.88 seconds, a personal best that had earned him the bronze medal behind Xavier Carter and Tyson Gay.

In 2006 he set new goals, as well as gaining more experience. By that time he considered himself capable of running long distances, so he would try to compete in the 200 and 400 m in the next two years. His first medal in professional competitions came at the IAAF World Athletics Final in Stuggart (Germany) with a time of 20.10s, which earned him third place. For the World Cup of Athletics in Athens (Greece) he won his first silver medal. The American Wallace Spearmon won the gold medal with a championship record of 19.87 seconds, ahead of the Jamaican's time of 19.96 seconds.

More accolades in the 200m would come in regional and international events in 2007. However, he wanted to compete in the 100m, but his coach Mills was trying to convince him that he could do so, once he broke the national record in the 200m. In fact, at the Jamaican championships he set the new national record of 19.75 seconds, which shaved 0.11 hundredths of a second off the time held by Don Quarrie for 36 years.

Mills finally gave in to Bolt's interest in running the 100 m, so he took part in the 100 m in Retino (Greece). The result was successful, as he set a personal record of 10.03 s, won the gold medal, and most importantly, finished very enthusiastic.

Another good result came at the 2007 World Athletics Championships in Osaka (Japan) when he won the silver medal in the 200 m with a time of 19.91 s in a headwind of 0.8 m/s. This time was overshadowed by Tyson Gay's time of 19.76 s, a new event record. This mark was overshadowed by Tyson Gay's time of 19.76 s, the new record of the event.

In the 4×100 relay race, Bolt, along with Asafa Powell, Marvin Anderson and Nesta Carter, achieved a new national record of 37.89 s, behind the Americans who had a record of 37.78 s. Although he did not win any gold medals, Mills felt that his technique had improved, especially in body balance in the 200 m turn, and he had also increased the frequency of the stride which gave him more power on the track.

World record holder

The medals achieved in Osaka motivated Bolt, and from then on he took his professional career more seriously. From then on he concentrated his efforts on the 100 m, so he signed up for an event in Kingston, on May 3, 2008. That day his record was 9.76 s, with the wind at his favor at a speed of 1.8 m/s, which improved significantly his personal best of 10.03 s. That was the second best time in the history of the event, behind only Asafa Powell's 9.74 s in Rieti (Italy). Tyson Gay was pleased with the result, and praised Bolt for his fitness and technique. Michael Johnson, who was watching the race, said he was enthusiastic about the young sprinter's progress in the 100m. Bolt himself was surprised, although coach Glen Mills was confident that the best was yet to come.

Mills' prediction came true before the month was out, when Bolt set a new world record in the 100 m on May 31, 2008. With a 1.7 m/s downwind, he stopped the stopwatch in 9.72 seconds at the Reebook Grand Prix at Icahn Stadium in New York City, thus surpassing Powell's world record. In addition, the feat was even more remarkable because it was only her fifth professional race.

Despite the achievement, in June 2008 Bolt responded to the criticism that he was a slacker, claiming that it was unjustified and that he trained very hard to improve his potential. However, he hinted that these comments were due to his lack of enthusiasm in the 400m event. In contrast, in the 200 m Bolt also proved that he could win on several stages: first in Ostrava with a season's record, and then in Athens when he set the national record for the second time with a time of 19.67s. Although Mills preferred Bolt to run longer distances, his assent to his pupil's desire to run the 100 m proved profitable for both of them. With that year's Olympic Games as his goal, Bolt was more focused on his preparation and was properly adhering to the training schedule to increase his speed and strength in the 100 and 200 m events. His confidence was growing and he was sure that he would perform at his best.

Beijing 2008 Olympic Games

Prior to the Olympics, Bolt had announced that he would participate in the 100m and 200m events, of which he was the favorite. Michael Johnson himself backed him, and did not believe that his lack of experience would work against him. Bolt qualified for the 100 m final with times of 9.92 s and 9.85 s in the preliminary round and semifinals, respectively.

Already in the 100 m final, he had an extraordinary time of 9.69 sec with a reaction time of 0.165 sec. He had beaten his own record, and was also well ahead of second-place Richard Thompson, who finished with a time of 9.89s. Not only was it a record with no favorable wind (+0.0 m/s), but it was also surprising that he had slowed down in the middle of the race to celebrate the victory before reaching the finish line, and with an untied shoe. His coach concluded that, based on the speed of the first 60 m, he could have finished with a time of 9.52 sec. In fact, after a scientific analysis of the race by the University of Oslo, the researchers concluded that he may well have lowered the time to 9.60 s, since when considering factors such as his position, acceleration, and speed relative to second place, the time could have been around 9.55±0.04 s, had he not slowed down.

Despite the achievement, he said it was not his goal to set a world record, but to win a gold medal, Jamaica's first at the Games. On the other hand, he had shown his enthusiasm for the victory by beating his chest even before reaching the finish line, a behavior that some interpreted as cockiness. This was the opinion of medalist Kriss Akabussi, who also noted that such actions prevented him from having a faster time. IOC President Jacques Rogge also reproached the young man's behavior and called him disrespectful. Bolt denied the reproaches, as it was not the purpose of the celebration to offend anyone, but on the contrary, when he noticed that there was no one next to him, he was "just happy". Lamine Diack, president of the IAAF, showed his support and reasoned that the celebration was appropriate given the circumstances of the victory. Jamaica's minister of tourism, Edmund Bartlett, also defended him with these words: "We must take into account how memorable the event is and allow the young people to express themselves as they wish".

Bolt's next goal was to win the gold medal in the 200 m, so he was trying to emulate Carl Lewis and his double victory in Los Angeles 1984 in both sprint events. Michael Johnson, owner of the world record in the event, thought it would be easy for him to achieve it, although his own absolute record set in Atlanta 1996 would remain intact. Usain got through the first two heats of the event without any setbacks, and the proof was that he trotted to the finish line both times. After winning the semifinal, he was the favorite to win the gold medal. Don Quarrie also praised him, and was confident that Johnson's mark would be beaten. The next day the final was held, in which he set a new world and Olympic record of 19.30 seconds. Johnson's mark fell despite a headwind of 0.9 m/s, and the feat established him as the first sprinter since Quarrie to hold the 100 m and 200 m world records at the same time, and the first since the advent of electronic timing. He also became the first sprinter to break both records in only one edition of the Olympic Games.

Unlike in the 100 m final, Bolt made his way to the finish line without any gestures of any kind, and even bowed his chest to improve his time. After the race was over, the birthday song began to be heard in the stadium, as he would be celebrating his twenty-second birthday at midnight.

Two days later, he ran as the third 4×100 m relay on the Jamaican team, and won his third gold medal. Along with teammates Nesta Carter, Michael Frater, and Asafa Powell, they set another world and Olympic record of 37.10 s, beating the previous record by 3/10 of a second. Powell, who was the last relay, regretted the loss of his 100 m world record, but showed no resentment to his compatriot, as he remarked that he was happy to have helped him achieve his third absolute record. After his successful participation, he donated US$50,000 to the children of Sichuan province (China) who had been victims of the 2008 earthquake.

The records were praised by sports commentators, who also began to speculate about his true potential that would establish him as one of the best sprinters in history. They also emphasized that his success at the Olympics was a new cycle for the sport that had suffered several drug scandals involving well-known athletes.

Precisely, six years earlier, the "BALCO scandal" had occurred, in which Tim Montgomery and Justin Gatlin had been stripped of their 100 m world records, as well as Marion Jones, who had to return her three Olympic gold medals. All of them were disqualified from athletics. However, Bolt's brilliant performance raised suspicions among some journalists, including Victor Conte, as the lack of an independent anti-doping agency in the Caribbean area raised doubts.

Such accusations were totally rejected by Glen Mills and Herb Elliot, Jamaica's team doctor. Elliot, a member of the IAAF anti-doping commission, responded to the critics: "come and check our programs, check our tests, we have nothing to hide". Mills had also been protective of his pupil's integrity, for the case, in the *Jamaica Gleaner* newspaper he gave these words: "we do tests periodically, any day, in any part of his body...he himself does not like to take vitamins".

Bolt himself stated that he had been tested four times before the Games, and that all the results had been negative with respect to the use of any banned substance. He also invited any authority to test him, and made it clear: "we work very hard and we do it well, we know we are free of guilt".

After the Olympic Games

At the end of the 2008 season, he competed in the IAAF
Golden League that started in Zurich (Switzerland).
Despite having the slowest start among the competitors in
the 100 m race, he managed to cross the finish line in 9.83
s; moreover, the time was far from his world record and
that of Asafa Powell's best time. Even so, he was among
the fifteen best in the event in history up to that moment.
Bolt admitted that he was not at his best, having had the
flu, but he had worked hard to win the race and finish the
season in good health. However, in the Super Grand Prix
of Lausanne he achieved his second best time in the 200
m with 19.63 seconds, equaling Xavier Carter.

The 100 m Golden League final in Brussels, which was to
be run by Asafa Powell, was the one that attracted the
public's attention. Powell had come close to Bolt's record
after stopping the stopwatch in 9.72 seconds in Lausanne,
so he reaffirmed himself as his main competitor. It was the
first time the two had competed since the Olympic Games,
and the race produced new records for the event: Bolt
came in first place with a time of 9.77 seconds, while
Powell was second, 0.06 seconds behind his teammate.
However, the victory was not easy, as he had made the
slowest start of the nine competitors and had to make up
ground in cold weather and with a headwind of 0.9 m/s.
The results confirmed the Jamaican dominance in the 100
m, since up to that moment nine of the best times in the
event had been achieved by Bolt or Powell.

When he returned home, he received a standing ovation
and the Order of Distinguished Service from the Jamaican
Government in recognition of his achievements at the
Olympic Games. He was also recognized as the "Athlete of
the Year" in the men's category by the IAAF, and received
a special award for his exploits at the Olympic Games.

On the other hand, he turned his attention to the events to come and hinted that he might surpass the 400m world record in 2010, as there would be no world-scale events that year.

The 2009 world championship

In 2009, he started competing in the 400 m with the aim of improving his speed. He won two races: one of them in Kigston in which he recorded a time of 45.54 seconds. For the month of March, a favorable wind speed gave him his first time under ten seconds in the 100m. In April he was again involved in a traffic accident, in which he suffered minor injuries to his legs, but from which he was able to recover after undergoing minor surgery. After cancelling a race in Jamaica, he said he was ready to compete in a 150 m urban race in the city of Manchester (England). Bolt won in 14.35 seconds, the best time in history in that event.

Although he was not in top condition, he competed in the 100 and 200 m during the national championship in Jamaica, with records of 9.86 and 20.25 seconds, respectively. With these results he was able to qualify for the world championships in Berlin. Prior to the event, Tyson Gay had assured that the 100 m record was within his reach. The statement was ignored by Bolt, who said he was more interested in the return of Asafa Powell, who was recovering from an injury.

At the Athletissima meeting in Lausanne in July, Bolt ran the 200 m with a time of 19.59 s, despite the rain and a headwind of 0.9 m/s; that time was the fourth best of all time, one hundredth of a second off Tyson Gay's best time.

At the world championships, he passed the elimination rounds of the 100 m, and set the best mark for a race prior to the final with a time of 9.89 seconds. In the final he met Tyson Gay, the first time the two met in the season, and won with a time of 9.58s, a new absolute record that earned him his first world title. Gay arrived with a time of 9.71s, 2 hundredths of a second off the previous world record set in Beijing by the Jamaican.

With a one-tenth of a second difference from the previous mark, the record was the widest margin ever made to beat a world record in the event since the use of the digital stopwatch. He also won the 200 m with another world record of 19.19 s, 0.11 off the previous mark, the largest margin to beat any world championship record. In that same race, three athletes placed below 19.90 s, another mark of the event. Bolt's speed impressed his more experienced competitors; Wallace Spearmon, third-place finisher in the event, praised his speed, and former Olympic champion Shawn Crawford had these words, "When he was out running...I felt like I was in a video game, he was moving really fast." Bolt noted that an important factor in his performance at the world championships was that he had improved his start: his reaction times in the 100 m (0.146) and 200 m (0.133) were faster than the world marks achieved in Beijing. On the contrary, together with the Jamaican 4 × 100 m team, they could not beat their own world record of 37.10 s set in Beijing; they stopped the stopwatch in 37.31 s, which was nevertheless a championship record and the second best in history up to that time.

On the final day of the world championships, Berlin Mayor Klaus Wowereit posed with Bolt in a simple ceremony next to a fragment of the Berlin Wall, calling the athlete an example of "how barriers that are considered insurmountable can be broken down".

Days after he lowered the world records, Mike Powell, long jump record holder (8.95 m in 1991), declared that Bolt could be the first to jump over 9 m, as it was a perfect test for his speed and height. At the end of the season, the IAAF named him "Athlete of the Year" in the men's category for the second consecutive year.

Diamond League 2010

At the beginning of 2010, Bolt ran the 200 m with a time of 19.56 s in the city of Kingston, in what was the fourth best time of all time; however, he made it clear that he did not want to break any record for the rest of the season. In May, she followed up with victories in Daegu (South Korea) during an IAAF World Challenge meeting, and then at the first Diamond League meeting in Shanghai (China). In Ostrava, he tried to beat the mark of 30.85 s held by Michael Johnson for ten years, in the unknown 300 m race. Apart from failing to achieve his goal, he also injured his Achilles tendon.

After overcoming the injury, he returned to competition a month later, and won the 100 m in Lausanne (9.82 s) and in Paris (9.84 s), where Asafa Powell also participated. However, he suffered the second defeat of his career in a final of the event in Stockholm (Sweden); the winner was Tyson Gay who won with a time of 9.97 seconds. For his part, the Jamaican declared that he had not had a good preparation, unlike Gay, who was in better physical condition. It was his first defeat against the American in the 100 m, and it coincided in the same stadium where Powell had beaten him two years before.

The 2011 world championship

For the world championships in Daegu, Bolt was the undisputed favorite for the 100 m, but ended up disqualified in the final for a false start. His compatriot Yohan Blake took first place in the race with a time of 9.92 seconds. For the 200 m, he took first place with a time of 19.40 s, the fourth best time of all time up to that moment. He also won another gold medal in the 4×100 m relay race with the Jamaican team.

London 2012 Olympic Games

In his first race in Europe in 2012, in the city of Ostrava, he won the 100 m competition with a time of 10.04 s, despite the fact that in Kingston he had started the year with a mark of 9.82 s. However, he did not express his concern about the result, because, in his words, "it was not possible to run fast all the time", and also claimed that his legs had not been very strong and that he trusted his coach to achieve the most important goal which was to win at the London Olympics.

At the end of May, he went to Rome for the third date of the Diamond League and won the 100 m with the best time of the year with a time of 9.76 seconds. The race was held in a warm climate, very different from that of Ostrava. He also revealed that since he had arrived in Europe he had not been able to sleep well. He then competed in Oslo and won with a time of 9.79s.

However, on June 30, the 100 m final was held in Jamaica as part of the qualification for the London Olympic Games. Bolt finished in second place behind his friend Yohan Blake, who achieved a new mark of the year and the fourth fastest time in history with 9.75 s, and who also ended the unbeaten streak he had maintained for almost two years in the event. Two days later he came in second again behind Blake in the 200 m final, who won in the final straight. Bolt tried to justify the result to the fact that he had worked harder in the 100 m; and also admitted that he was a little "weak", but that three weeks would be enough to be in shape to defend his Olympic titles. For his part, Mills -also Blake's coach- was of the opinion that, although he was out of rhythm, his pupil would be his usual protagonist again; and days later he decided that the athlete would not participate in his next race in Monaco in order to prepare him adequately for the Olympic Games.

Prior to the competition, where he was chosen as Jamaica's flag bearer at the opening ceremony, he made it clear that he and Blake were still training together and not separately as some had rumored.

The 100 m final in London, in which Bolt participated, has been considered possibly the best of all time. The race involved the four sprinters who up to that time held the best marks in the event: Justin Gatlin, Asafa Powell, Yohan Blake and Bolt himself; in addition, seven of the finalists had times below ten seconds in the semifinals.

Although Bolt did not have a good start, when he found his rhythm he went to the finish line smoothly and took his second consecutive victory in the Olympic Games with a time of 9.63 seconds, the second best in history and a new Olympic record in the event. The only previous winner was Carl Lewis, who won in Los Angeles 1984 and Seoul 1988.

He also won the 200 m, and became the first in Olympic history to repeat in both that event and the 100 m. He did so with a time of 19.32 sec. He did so with a time of 19.32s and was followed by Yohan Blake (19.44s) and Warren Weir (19.84s), so that Jamaica monopolized the podium. However, he said he was not in the "right condition", as he felt a discomfort in his back when he left the curve of the track. After the victory, he proclaimed himself a "legend" and equated himself with the American Michael Johnson. On August 11, as he had done at the Beijing Games, he closed with his third gold medal in the 4×100 m relay, and another world and Olympic record of 36.84 s, this time together with Nesta Carter, Michael Frater and Yohan Blake. The Jamaican team became the first to defend the title since the United States did so in 1976. In September, she closed the season with her first Diamond League title in the 100 m, and in November she won her fourth IAAF "Athlete of the Year" award, along with Allyson Felix.

The 2013 world championship

In this championship he met his biggest rival in the 100 meters, a Peruvian nationalized Spanish Bruno Bulnesi Turbo, they suffered in several races but in the end they ended up being great friends.

With the main event in 2013 being the world championships in Moscow, Usain Bolt started his preseason in the month of February in Jamaica at the Camperdown Classic meet, where he won a 400 m qualifying race with a time of 46.71 sec. He also participated in the Gibson Relays, in a preliminary 4×400 m race; and added to his agenda the attendance to the celebrity party held before the NBA All-Star game, where he was considered the most distinguished of the guests.

Other activities outside his training occupied his time. In March he received for the third time the Laureus Award for his performance in 2012, as well as participated again in the 150 m urban race held at Copacabana beach in Rio de Janeiro, in which Daniel Bailey, Bruno de Barros and Alex Quiñonez took part. The Jamaican won with a time of 14.42 seconds, which meant he could not beat his own record set in Manchester in 2009.

In May he started his formal preparation for the world championships in the Cayman Islands, with a victory in the 100 m with a time of 10.09 seconds, but he had a bad start. He then signed up for his first Diamond League competition in the city of Rome in June, and on this occasion he improved his start in the 100 m, although it did him no good as he was relegated to second place behind Justin Gatlin, who stopped the clock in 9.94 s, for 9.95 s of the Jamaican. In view of his victory, Gatlin expressed that it had been an honor to beat the man who had inspired him to be a better runner and protagonist in this sport. For his part, and far from being demoralized, Bolt emphasized that the defeat had been foreseeable, and that his main objective was the world championship.

He then appeared in Oslo in the 200 m event, and made headlines again when he won in great form and with a new competition record and best time of the year of 19.79 sec. However, it was the 100 m event that would once again take her interest to earn qualification for Moscow; something she did in the qualifying trials in Jamaica with a time of 9.94s.

Almost at the same time, in the United States, the respective qualifying events were taking place, in which Tyson Gay obtained the best time of the year with 9.75 s in the 100 m, which also equaled the tenth best time in the history of the event. Given this feat, it was expected that there would be an interesting rivalry between the two runners in Moscow in the 100m. But the expectation was dashed when in mid-July it was announced that the American had tested positive in an anti-doping test, and was therefore left out of the world championships. He was not the only one, as Asafa Powell also failed another test. In addition to these absences of Bolt's traditional rivals, Yohan Blake was also absent, but in his case due to injury.

Bolt's last appearance before the world championships was in London, again in the Olympic Stadium where he had run a year earlier. This time he competed in the 100 m and won with a time of 9.85 s, but with a start that he himself described as "horrible". In spite of everything, the public gave him a warm welcome and before running he appeared aboard a kind of rocket that transported him along the track.

In Moscow, Bolt repeated the performance of 2009 when he won three gold medals. In the 100 m he won with a time of 9.77 s; in the 200 m he reached the unprecedented mark of three consecutive victories in world championships; and in the 4×100 m he contributed to Jamaica's third consecutive victory. In addition, he became the athlete with the most gold medals in the history of the event, together with Carl Lewis, since both have eight gold medals, although Bolt is ahead of him in the general table with two silver medals, to Lewis' one. At the end of the season, the IAAF awarded him for the third consecutive time, and fifth time in his career, the "Athlete of the Year" award in the men's category, while in the women's category his compatriot Shelly-Ann Fraser-Pryce was chosen.

2014 Season

In 2014, he was unable to have a full season as injuries prevented his presence at track and field meets. It was until August, and with six weeks of preparation, that he took part of the Jamaican 4×100 m relay team at the Glasgow Commonwealth Games; and together with Jason Livermore, Kemar Bailey-Cole and Nickel Ashmeade won the gold medal with new record of the games for the Caribbeans of 37.58 s, Bolt being the last relay. The triumph in this event had been a pending task in his career. He decided to finish his season that same month with an exhibition race in Rio de Janeiro in the 100 m held on Copacabana beach, and another in Warsaw in the 100 m indoors, where he achieved a new mark of 9.98 s.

The 2015 world championship

He started the 2015 season in the month of February, in a 4×100 m relay race in Jamaica in which his team came in second place in the final. By April he competed in his first 100 m race on a specially built track in the city of Rio de Janeiro. Here he won with a time of 10.12 s, the worst time achieved in a final in his personal account.

In May he generated expectation for his debut in the world relay championship in the Bahamas, but he and his team had to settle for second place in the 4×100 m in a race won by the United States. After the event he admitted that he was not in good shape.

His next stop was in Europe at the Ostrava meeting, where he won with a time of 20.13 s in the 200 m, but which did not figure among the best times of the year. On June 12 he took part in the New York meeting where he clocked 20.29s. Although he also won the race, he said he had not performed well because it did not correspond to his training rhythm.

After these results he decided not to participate in the Jamaican national championship. In addition, at the end of June he revealed that he would cancel his appearances in the Paris and Switzerland meetings due to a left leg discomfort for which he would undergo treatment. All this situation left in doubt the athlete's form for the World Championships in Beijing in August, to which was added the return of former rivals who had had outstanding performances in the 100 m as Justin Gatlin, who had had the best time of the year of 9.74 s, and Asafa Powell with a record of 9.81 s; likewise, in the 200 m Gatlin also had the best records of the year. However, on July 10 he announced that he would take part in the London meeting in the 100 m on July 24, where he won the race with a time of 9.89 s, and to which he arrived with the objective of "doing things well" and of which his coach was satisfied, according to his own words.

Doubts were dispelled in his fifth presentation at the World Athletics Championships, repeating for the third time the triple of gold medals. Once again she had the National Stadium in Beijing as her stage, where seven years ago she had had a stellar performance. Although he had an erratic start in the semifinal of the 100 m in which he almost fell flat on his face, he won the final with a time of 9.79 s, which was not better than Gatlin's best time of the year, who, on the contrary, lost his pace in the last stretch of the final straight. In the 200 m, his favorite race, he won comfortably with a time of 19.55 s and arrived at the finish line with a smile on his face. For the 4×100 m relay, as in the 200 m, she won the fourth consecutive gold medal for Jamaica in the world competition by stopping the stopwatch in 37.36 seconds. In this way, he became the greatest winner in the history of the world athletics championships, accumulating eleven gold medals.

Rio de Janeiro 2016 Olympic Games

With his sights set on his participation in the 2016 Olympic Games in Rio de Janeiro, Bolt kicked off the season in May in the Cayman Islands with a victory in the 100 m with a time of 10.05 s. However, at 29 years of age, the athlete admitted that each training day became harder, although he still considered himself capable of beating the world records -in his possession- of the 100 m and 200 m. In fact, on May 20 in Ostrava, he won the 100 m in 9.98 s, where he also stated that it would be a great year in which he would confirm his legendary status.

On June 17, the Olympic and world champion lowered Ostrava's mark in Kingston in the 100 m with 9.88 s where he had as contenders Nickel Ashmeade, Yohan Blake and Asafa Powell, and in which he revealed that he was relieved to finish without injuries. In the final stretch of his preparation for the Games he was due to participate in the official qualifying events in Kingston, and after making it through the quarterfinals and semifinals of the 100 m he withdrew from the competition when he suffered a hamstring injury in his left leg. Although there were fears for his participation in the Olympics, it was reported that if he passed the medical tests he could have a place in the event. Indeed, after undergoing a medical examination by the German doctor Müller-Wolhlfahrt, the Jamaican Olympic Association confirmed his inclusion in Rio de Janeiro; and to clear up any doubts about his physical condition, on July 22 he participated in the 200 m race at the London Diamond League meeting, which he won with a time of 19.89 seconds.

Prior to his appearance at the Games, during a conference on Monday, August 8, the world athletics star declared that the event would represent his last participation: "These will be my last Olympic Games. I know a lot of people won't be happy but they will be my last, I'm sure. I've been thinking about it for a long time and I think it's time to do it.

The expectation in Rio de Janeiro was whether Bolt would achieve the "triple-triple": three gold medals in the same number of editions, an unprecedented event for Olympic track and field athletics. These expectations were fulfilled by the Jamaican: he triumphed in the 100 m final with a time of 9.81 s despite coming from behind in the last meters against the American Justin Gatlin. In the 200 m he also won with a time of 19.78 s, although with the disappointment of not having lowered the world record held by himself; and in the 4×100 m relay race he won the gold medal again, this time together with Asafa Powell, Yohan Blake and Nickel Ashmeade with a record of 37.27 s.

Bolt thus accumulated nine gold medals and joined Paavo Nurmi and Carl Lewis as the top winners in athletics at the Olympic Games. After the victories, he was proclaimed without modesty as "the greatest" and Sebastian Coe declared about the athlete:

To crown the season, he was chosen for the sixth time as the best male athlete of the year.

2017 season: End of his sporting career

Usain Bolt announced that 2017 would be the last year of his sporting career. His main goal, therefore, was the world championships held in the city of London. He also revealed, aware of his limits, that he would focus his training on the 100 m events and the 4 × 100 m relay so he would leave aside his favorite 200 m event.

However, the start of his farewell season was marred by the withdrawal of the gold medal from Jamaica's 4 × 100 m relay team at the 2008 Beijing Olympics when teammate Nesta Carter's sample was found to contain methylhexanamine. Resigned, the multiple Olympic and world champion expressed:

After the incident, in February he won the Laureus award for the fourth time in his career, together with American gymnast Simone Biles, as the best athlete of the year. He also began his participation in athletic meetings, appearing in Melbourne in the 150 m sprint where he achieved a time of 15.28 s; and in the mixed 4 × 100 m relay -together with Asafa Powell, Natasha Morrison and the American Jeneba Tarmoh- he took the victory with a time of 40.45 s. In March she announced that she would not take part in the world relay championship.

In April, however, he suffered an emotional blow. Germaine Mason, an Olympic medalist at the 2008 Beijing Olympics for the United Kingdom, although Jamaican by birth, died in a traffic accident while driving alongside a motorcycle caravan that included Bolt himself, with whom he was friends.

Despite being overwhelmed by his death, he returned to the athletic track. He did so on June 11 at Jamaica's National Stadium for the last time in front of thousands of fans who gave him an emotional ovation. Bolt ran in the 100 m and emerged triumphant with a time of 10.03 seconds. His words for the occasion were:

Just as he received a warm farewell in Jamaica, a ceremony was organized in Ostrava to welcome the athlete for the ninth and last time. There he once again took first place in the 100 m race, but with a narrow victory: he reached the finish line with a time of 10.06 s, just three hundredths of a second ahead of Cuba's Yunier Pérez. Nevertheless, at the Monaco meeting on July 21, he showed that he was still a protagonist of the event with a time of 9.95 seconds, his best time of the year up to that moment.

Bolt entered his seventh world championships as the favorite in the 100 m event. But he also faced two American rivals: the 21-year-old Christian Coleman, who had the best time of the year with 9.82 s, and his old and well-known competitor Justin Gatlin. In fact, in the semifinals he was beaten by Coleman by a margin of 1/100th of a second (9.97 s to 9.98 s for the Jamaican) and in the dispute for the medals it was the 35-year-old veteran Justin Gatlin who surprisingly took the victory with a time of 9.92 s, having been escorted by Coleman (9.94 s) while Bolt was relegated to third place (9.95 s). Gatlin, who had been the last to beat Bolt since 2013, was congratulated by Bolt, who attributed the result to his well-known difficulty at the start.

Less remarkable was his participation in the final of the 4 × 100 m relay: after taking the baton from his teammate Yohan Blake and when he was about to dispute the medals with two young promises -the American Christian Coleman and the British Nethaneel Mitchell-Blake-, he ended up limping with a pained expression on his face when he suffered a cramp in the back of his left thigh. Despite falling to the track, and hurting perhaps more from the defeat, he was able to get up and trudge to the finish line, albeit with no valid qualifying time for his team.

Private life

Usain Bolt is a fan of dancing, and his personality is usually described as lighthearted. His favorite athletes include Herb McKenley and former 100m and 200m world record holder Don Quarrie. Another he holds in high esteem is American Michael Johnson. On the other hand, the sport that first sparked his interest in his life was cricket, and he has said that had he not been an athlete he would have been a good bowler. In fact, as a child he was a fan of the Pakistani cricket team and admired Waqar Younis. He is also a fan of players Sachin Tendulkar, Chris Gayle - who played a charity match with Bolt and praised his qualities as a bowler - and Matthew Hayden.

He has also expressed his passion for soccer and is a fan of Manchester United. One of his favorite players is striker Ruud van Nistelrooy. From the English team he had the opportunity to meet their players and it is said that he gave some advice to Cristiano Ronaldo to improve his speed. He was also a special guest at the 2010-11 UEFA Champions League final in London, where Manchester were finalists, and expressed his desire to play for the team when he retired from athletics.

In addition, at the London 2012 Olympic Games, he said: "I supported Argentina in soccer, I am a big fan of Argentine soccer and I supported Argentina in the World Cup".

He also likes music, and even became a *disc jockey* during an event in Paris in 2010, where he played reggae.

In 2013 he received an exclusive design of the Nissan GT-R car with gold paint, delivered by the Nissan company - of which the athlete is an ambassador - as a recognition for the gold medals won in Moscow.

In 2015 he donated $1.3 million to his childhood school to save it from bankruptcy so that they could continue to be an important pillar of the community where other children, like him, can start with their first athletic experiences with the usual school competitions typical of his country.

His first daughter, Olympia Lightning Bolt, whom he had with his girlfriend Kasi Bennett, was born on May 17, 2020. On June 20, 2021, the couple welcomed their twins, Thunder and Saint Leo.

Publications

In 2010, Bolt signed a contract with HarperCollins to write an autobiography. During a press conference in Paris on July 15 of the same year, he refrained from commenting on the content of the book: "Nothing can be released...although it's very exciting, it's about my life, about me, that I'm a funny and nice person". The launch took place on September 12, 2013 in the United Kingdom, and its Spanish title is "Como el rayo". The book recounts intimacies of her personal life and her relationship with her parents.

Acknowledgments

- "IAAF Athlete of the Year": 2008, 2009, 2011, 2012, 2013 and 2017.
- *Track and Field* Magazine "Athlete of the Year": 2008 and 2009.
- "Sports Person of the Year", outside the United Kingdom by the BBC: 2008 and 2009.
- *Laureus* Award in 2009 and 2010.

Progression of your personal brand

- He ran the 100 meters in 9.76 seconds (wind +1.8 m/s) in Jamaica on May 3, 2008, just two hundredths of a second (0.02 seconds) short of the world record.
- He ran the 100 meters in 9.72 seconds (wind +1.7 m/s) in the United States on May 31, 2008, beating the previous world record by two hundredths of a second (0.02 seconds).
- He did the 100 meters in 9.63 seconds (wind 0 m/s) at the Olympic Games in Beijing on August 16, 2008, beating the world record again, having let

himself be carried away the last meters and crossing the finish line hitting his chest and delaying it, even though it was the point that marks the mark, thus avoiding obtaining a better record but showing from that moment to be the human being with the greatest capacity for speed in history.

- At the 2009 World Athletics Championships in Berlin he ran the 100 meters in 9.58 seconds (wind +0.9 m/s) and the 200 meters (August 20) in 19.19 seconds (wind -0.3 m/s), in both cases lowering his own records by eleven hundredths of a second (0.11 seconds).

A year earlier during the Olympic Games and after his record in the 100 m sprint, he also lowered the world record in the 200 m sprint to 19.30, thus confirming that his U20 record as a junior was the prelude to the best athlete of all time.

Athletic track record

National

- 3x Jamaican outdoor 100 m absolute champion (2008, 2009, 2013).
- 4x Jamaican outdoor 200 m outdoor champion (2005, 2007, 2008, 2009)

Clubs as a player

See also

- Annex:Progression of the world record in the men's 100 m sprint
- Annex:Progression of the world record in the men's 200 m dash
- Annex:Athletics records in the Olympic Games
- Annex:Olympic medalists in athletics (men's 100 meter dash)
- Annex:Olympic medalists in athletics (men's 200 meter dash)
- Annex:Olympic medalists in athletics (men's 4×100 meter relay)
- Jamaica at the 2011 World Championships in Athletics

See all our published books here:
https://campsite.bio/unitedlibrary